THE CUP OF · DESTINY

JANE LYLE

THE CUP OF ·DESTINY·

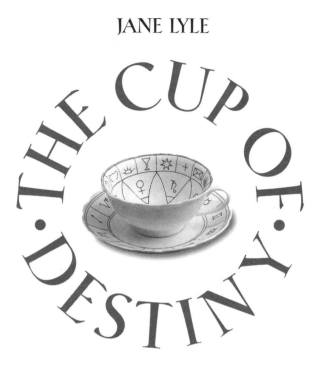

Traditional fortune–telling from tea leaves

BARNES
&NOBLE
BOOKS
NEW YORK

For my mother and grandmother, without whom a cup of tea would have been far less interesting.

With love and thanks.

PLEASE NOTE: The *Cup of Destiny* cup and saucer that were created to accompany this book are hand decorated, and therefore not dishwasher safe. We recommend that you wash them carefully by hand.

This edition published by Barnes and Noble, Inc.,
by arrangement with Eddison Sadd Editions

2000 Barnes & Noble Books

M 10 9 8 7 6 5 4 3 2

ISBN 0-7607-2267-6

Published by arrangement with
Eddison ◆ Sadd Editions Limited
St Chad's Court
148 King's Cross Road
London
WC1X 9DH

Phototypeset in Phaistos using QuarkXPress on Apple Macintosh
Origination by Pixel Graphics, Singapore
Printed and bound by Leo Paper Products, China

Contents

Introduction

This book is designed to introduce you to the intimate and delightful art of divination by tea leaves or coffee grounds.

This charming skill, more correctly known as 'tasseography', is the direct descendant of an Ancient Greek practice. Consulting the patterns made by wine sediments tossed into a metal bowl, the process – known as 'olchromancy' – was a widespread, popular method in a culture that revered omens and symbols, and found them everywhere. In largely non-literate societies, visual symbols play the role of storyteller, seer, guide and counsellor, a role it is hard for us to fully understand. But we can rediscover and reawaken this submerged part of ourselves, and so enhance our natural intuition and awareness. Divination by tea leaves or coffee grounds is, of course,

only a few centuries old since these beverages were not available in the West, and even when they were imported were extremely expensive and luxurious. During the eighteenth and nineteenth centuries tea and coffee drinking became more common, and by the mid-nineteenth century, this form of fortune-telling was well-established all over Europe and the Middle East.

And, whimsical though it seems, it has survived because it can be effective.

But how can such an apparently random method produce results? It is easy to be sceptical about something which seems so unlikely, almost primitive. However, the rational mind cannot see pictures in clouds or faces peering out from rock formations, while to the eye of an artist or a child the whole world is alive with unexpected images. Reading the cup is just the same, it is the difference between looking and really seeing with the imagination.

Great artists know about this vital difference, as a brief extract from Leonardo da Vinci's notebooks makes clear:

'I cannot forbear to mention ... a new device for study which, although it may seem trivial and almost ludicrous, is nevertheless extremely useful in arousing the mind to various inventions. And this is, when you look at a wall spotted with stains ... you may discover a resemblance to various landscapes, beautified with mountains, rivers, rocks, trees ... and an endless variety of objects which you could reduce to complete and well-drawn forms.'

The pictures and symbols in the cup reflect the hopes, dreams and concerns of the individual who consults this domestic oracle. Identifying them, and imbuing them with resonance and meaning requires imagination,

intuition and practice. The more you do it, the better your results will be – whether for yourself or others.

There is, perhaps, no more fascinating method, a method which blends a dash of mystery with a generous measure of common sense. It is deceptively simple, and utterly magical. I hope you enjoy learning how to do it as much as I did.

'To be shaken out of the ruts of ordinary perception, to be shown for a few timeless hours the outer and the inner world ... this is an experience of inestimable value to everyone.'

ALDOUS HUXLEY, *The Doors of Perception.*

May you always find fortune in your cup.

JANE LYLE

PART ONE

HOW TO MAKE A READING

This part of the book is designed to show you how to read tea leaves or coffee grounds in the traditional way, and also gives you instructions for the 'Cup of Destiny' fortune-telling game. You will enjoy experimenting with both methods, since a satisfying and illuminating reading can be obtained either way. However, those of you who are keen to develop and enhance your intuition may prefer the traditional method, which requires more effort from a beginner. Never try to combine these techniques, and decide in advance which one you are going to use for the best results.

Preparing for a Reading

Telling fortunes from tea leaves or coffee grounds is a simple yet effective divination technique, but attention to detail makes all the difference. To get the best results use loose tea: do not be tempted to cut open a teabag – the tea leaves will be too small and uniform in size to create varied patterns. Different blends of tea will also affect the patterns in your tea cup. A mix of Chinese and Indian tea is one of the most successful blends, or a speciality tea such as Earl Grey will often give pleasing results.

Make your tea in a pot, using this ritual as a moment to meditate on what you are doing, and clear your mind of mental clutter. Pour the tea without using a tea-strainer, and as you drink it focus on your question, or perhaps just the week ahead. If you are reading for a friend, tell them to concentrate briefly on current concerns, but there is no real need for lengthy reflection. Relaxation is more important. When the cup is almost empty, with just a little liquid left in the bottom, you are ready to begin:

1 Pick up your cup in your left hand (or your right if you are left-handed). Breathe deeply, close your eyes, and ask your question – if you have one. Otherwise, just ask the cup to reveal your

fortune in the week or month ahead. When you are ready, circle the cup three times in a counterclockwise direction (see below, left). You can count each circle out loud – 'one, two, three' – or note them mentally. We always counted the 'spins' aloud when I was growing up, but this is personal preference.

2 Turn the cup upside down on its saucer, and allow it to drain (see below, right). It is best to remain silent during this process, to create the right atmosphere and to mark it out as a special moment. After all, you are preparing to look into the future, and that can be quite a serious business.

3 Once you are satisfied that the cup has drained completely, turn it over, pick it up, and look at the patterns, shapes and symbols. What is your first impression? Is the cup overflowing with pictures or is it quite empty and clear? Don't even look for specific symbols just yet, but allow yourself to dream and drift a little as you consider the patterns before you.

4 Read the cup in a clockwise direction, beginning at the handle (see overleaf). The handle represents you, or your inquirer, and so the symbols closest to it are especially meaningful, often describing your current frame of mind or a dominant character trait.

Imminent events are found close by, near the rim. Always begin with an examination of this area, as it is key to the rest of the reading.

PARTS OF THE CUP

The cup divides into three sections:

- THE RIM AND UPPER PART
- THE MIDDLE AREA
- THE BASE OF THE CUP

THE RIM — represents the immediate present and future — perhaps a day or so.

THE MIDDLE — represents a little further into the future, up to a week ahead.

THE BASE — is further away, the end of the week or even a few months ahead. If a number appears in the bottom it often signifies a number of weeks or months before an important or meaningful event will occur. This could be up to six months or more in the future. Traditional readers say 'within a three', for example, meaning three weeks, months or possibly years before the event takes place. The event itself will be symbolized by a picture or shape appearing beside the number.

READING ITS SECRETS

Turn the cup this way and that until you discern meaningful pictures. Use the handle as your fixed point, remembering that it represents you. In this way you minimize confusion, and increase accuracy.

Never strain to make sense of a cup that refuses to divulge its secrets. It may not be the right time for a reading, or the week ahead could be dull and uneventful. Try again later or wait a day or so for better results.

Finally, relax and open up your mind to the myriad possibilities. Your common sense and good humor are the most important tools for successful divination. Have fun.

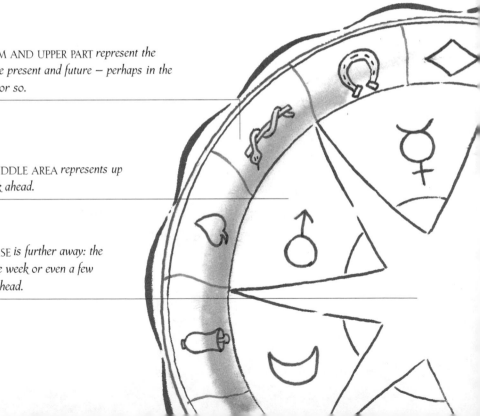

• THE RIM AND UPPER PART *represent the immediate present and future – perhaps in the next day or so.*

• THE MIDDLE AREA *represents up to a week ahead.*

• THE BASE *is further away: the end of the week or even a few months ahead.*

The *Cup of Destiny* Game

Your *Cup of Destiny* can be used in two ways. Its design is based on an antique original, with symbols and astrological glyphs – or symbols – which form the basis of a simple fortune-telling game, or serve to focus your mind on the world of imagination and intuition, a world you must enter if you want to glimpse the underlying patterns that shape our present and offer clues to our future. Beginners may find that using the cup to play this game is a creative and playful gateway into the realms of divination.

Once you are more confident, you can progress towards developing your own insights using the traditional interpretations and methods detailed in this book. You may prefer to use another, blank cup for this. Meanwhile, your *Cup of Destiny* is an amusement from the past that offers you a serious opportunity to exercise your imagination and intuition.

Prepare a pot of tea or freshly ground coffee; and pour a cup. As you drink, muse on your current concerns, or keep your mind blank. Step outside your everyday world, and clear your mind. Once you have nearly finished your drink, you can focus more specifically on a question, or ask the powers-that-be, your Higher Self, or guiding spirit, to reveal what the near future holds in store. If you are drinking coffee you could add a tiny pinch of fresh-ground beans to the liquid in the cup to ensure a satisfying pattern. Circle the cup three times counter-clockwise using your left hand and turn it over onto the saucer, allowing it to drain for several minutes before picking it up. Leaves or grounds will be distributed around the cup, the symbols they fall upon are the ones used to make a reading. Use the guide below to start making your own interpretations.

The symbols on the saucer represent the twelve signs of the zodiac, and you can learn more about these on pages 72–78.

WHAT THE SYMBOLS MEAN

The Rim

These symbols refer to the near future – usually the coming week or ten days. Sometimes events are up to a month away, but no more.

♦ ENVELOPE *A longed-for letter, or important document is on its way to you. It may contain good news.*

♦ EYE *A protective symbol in many cultures, the eye also hints at wonderful insights and new ways of looking at long-standing dilemmas.*

♦ ACE OF CLUBS *Practical matters, financial improvements, or even a gift will be significant.*

♦ BELL *Some happy news. Sometimes this means you will be making positive changes in your life.*

♦ ACE OF SPADES *Legal matters, official documents, large companies and serious commitments are all signified by this symbol. Actions and agreements made now could have a lasting or fateful effect on your future. Be thoughtful and cautious.*

◆ SNAKE *Someone does not deserve your trust. Be watchful, and do not confide in anyone you do not know well. If other warning signs appear (see* Ace of Spades *and* Cross*) keep quiet and guard your secrets well.*

◆ HORSESHOE *Fortunate coincidences, lucky breaks and meaningful surprises await you. Keep an open mind.*

◆ ACE OF DIAMONDS *An important time for your goals, ambitions and life direction. Expect positive developments and increased self-confidence.*

◆ ACE OF HEARTS *Love and romance are on the menu. This could mean spending time with your partner or the beginning of a new relationship. Your home life is also important to you now, which could signify a move, or making improvements on your current home.*

◆ CAT *Your independent streak and free spirit seek an outlet now, and you may feel like behaving unpredictably. Be adventurous and follow your heart.*

◆ SUNRISE *A new beginning, a sense of rebirth, or a fresh start are signified by this symbol.*

 ◆ CUP OR GLASS *Celebrations, parties and social invitations of every kind are indicated. Enjoy yourself!*

◆ STAR *Success in your projects, recognition and praise are all indicated. This is a lucky sign.*

◆ CROSS *A warning against overdoing it, taking on more than you can handle, or making impulsive mistakes by rushing things. Slow down and let go a little.*

The Inner Circle

Anyone familiar with astrology will recognize these as planetary symbols. Each planet traditionally signifies personal attributes and areas of life. These symbols deal with larger themes than those found around the rim, and refer to events over the coming weeks and months.

◆ **THE SUN** *You can make a positive impact on circumstances and people now. This symbol means creativity, joy and success.*

◆ **THE MOON** *Your innermost feelings, and most intimate relationships will be important. Pay attention to your dreams and intuitive inspiration.*

◆ **MARS** *Energy, action and assertiveness. Go for what you really want, unless other symbols advise against it.*

◆ **MERCURY** *Communication, conversations, travel and knowledge. This should be a social, lively phase.*

◆ **JUPITER** *Luck, expansion and heart–warming encounters brighten your life. Long–distance friendships or trips could broaden your horizons too.*

◆ **VENUS** *Love, art and harmony bring delightful interludes. You should be feeling creative and romantic.*

◆ **SATURN** *Self–discipline, responsibility, and plain hard work are needed now. You may face some kind of test, or need to make some area of your life more efficient.*

PART TWO

READING THE SIGNS

The following part of the book describes the most common symbols you are likely to find in your cup, and what they mean, according to my knowledge and understanding. Where symbols are cross-referenced, they appear in plain type (not italic), so you can check the index to see which pages they appear on.

Sooner or later you will see a picture of something I have not detailed; develop your intuition right from the start and you will be able to understand and interpret anything unusual. Similarly, if a particular symbol holds a special, personal meaning for you which does not agree with my interpretation, use your own meaning. Reading the cup is a personal and intuitive art. Trust yourself.

ABSTRACT SHAPES AND SYMBOLS

◆ **SQUARES OR RECTANGLES**
These usually foretell difficulties or challenges, but nothing too serious. However, there will be something to overcome or avoid in the near future. When there is something inside one of these shapes, it is likely to represent a letter or parcel with interesting contents. You may receive a gift or invitation, in the time zone indicated from its whereabouts in the cup.

◆ **DIAMOND** *Not only is the saying true that diamonds are a girl's best friend, a diamond is always a very positive symbol to discover in either a man or a woman's cup. Traditionally, this shape means you can look out for a gift of jewellery in the near future – just like the Ace of Diamonds in a deck of playing cards when they are used for fortune-telling. But this meaning can be stretched to include cash, surprise bonuses, windfalls and gifts in general. A diamond shape plus any money symbol would be very fortunate combination indeed.*

◆ **CIRCLE** *This must be clearly formed and have an unbroken, solid outline. They are fortunate symbols, suggesting money or gifts coming your way. A small circle could indicate a ring, meaning a gift or an offer of commitment, even marriage. Other symbols would confirm something as serious as a marriage proposal; never predict a wedding on the strength of a circle or ring alone. Nevertheless, whether a circle or ring is seen, this promises to be a positive and delightful phase.*

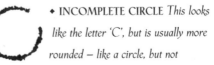

◆ **INCOMPLETE CIRCLE** *This looks like the letter 'C', but is usually more rounded – like a circle, but not*

completely closed. There will be an offer, but it is only a possibility at this time, and there is some way to go before it is definite or certain. Indeed, it may fall through, or change considerably before a conclusion or agreement can be reached. Faint circles, composed of tiny dots or 'tea dust' also represent tentative offers or questions that may not come to much in the end.

♦ TRIANGLE *Good luck from some unexpected source, or an uplifting experience of some kind. If it is found with negative symbols, such as rocks or dark clouds, the triangle means trouble from someone you trusted and admired. You may feel betrayed and disappointed. When found with a heart, the meaning is clear – a 'love triangle' is forming in your life. This may involve another person, or suggest that you or your partner are too involved with other matters to give much energy to your relationship. Interpret*

with great care, and never jump to conclusions or place negative ideas in someone's mind. See also entries for pyramid and wedge.

♦ WEDGE *A wedge is a triangle that is completely filled in with tea leaves or coffee grounds. And just as an actual wedge is used to hold a door open or shut, a symbolic wedge is somehow keeping things stuck in your life. Someone could be working against you without your knowledge, or may even be interfering in your love life. Adjacent symbols will reveal which area of your life is most affected, and whether you can or should confront the issue, now, or at a later date.*

♦ DOTS *Dots are commonly found in cups because of the nature of the leaves or grounds used in this fortune-telling method. So, look closely and see if they form a line, a circle, or any* other shape. A circle of dots means a trip of some kind, perhaps a holiday, perhaps a business trip. A line of dots also means a journey, but a short and inconsequential one. Many dots in a cup represent energy and vitality, a lively atmosphere surrounds you.

• **DASHES** *A number of short lines together suggest a period when you will be running around a lot more than usual, with a number of short trips and local journeys coming up. Some of these could be a waste of your time, so plan meticulously to avoid frustration and depleted energies.*

• **LINES** *Lines, like roads, mean movement and journeys. The clearer and straighter the line, the more rewarding the trip will be. Many lines could indicate the possibility of a job involving travel or a number of short trips for business or pleasure.*

• **WAVY LINE** *(see also river) A wavy line means emotions are running high, and you or your inquirer are particularly sensitive just now. When seen with signs of travel, a wavy line means a difficult or interrupted journey.*

• **ARROW** *Your direction in life is important when you see an arrow in the cup. Perhaps you are about to make a decision, and are wondering whether to make that leap into the unknown?*

An upward-pointing arrow (towards the rim of the cup) gives a resounding 'yes' to your question.

A straight arrow, pointing horizontally, means that nothing much will change as a result of your actions at this time.

An arrow pointing down to the bottom of the cup advises you to reconsider your options and think seriously about your aspirations and goals. You are heading in the wrong direction.

An arrow is also the symbol for the zodiac sign of Sagittarius. When linked to an initial, or sign, meaning a person, such as a head, a Sagittarian person could be important to you and your plans.

♦ SPIRAL Considerable energy accompanies this symbol, which signifies a lively mind and an inventive, creative phase. Rational analysis or logical thinking is unlikely to solve your problems now. What is needed are some intuitive quantum leaps, and you're in the right frame of mind to make them now.

♦ SPRIGS OR STICKS (tea only) Sprigs appear in tea cups sometimes; they are fragments of stems and more numerous in certain types of tea, such as Earl Grey or Chinese tea.

Sprigs and sticks generally represent people. If they appear to be vertical as you hold the cup to read it, they denote straightforward individuals. Sprigs lying across the cup; horizontally, warn of untrustworthy or dishonest people. My grandmother used to refer to these as 'a nasty leaf lying on its back'. Be cautious, especially if you see an offer or opportunity nearby. It might not be entirely what it seems initially.

A sprig or tea stick floating on a full cup of liquid is also meaningful, for it represents a visitor. Usually his or her arrival is imminent, the same day, or within two days of the reading.

♦ DROPS OF LIQUID While not strictly tea-leaf or coffee-ground symbols, drops of liquid are considered meaningful by many readers. In an otherwise well-drained cup they represent tears, and if there are several they were traditionally named 'tears and sobs'. Make sure you have allowed the cup to drain properly before interpreting this as a sign of sadness. However, when liquid clings stubbornly to the inside of the cup, and is coupled with other signs of unhappiness, it seems that you or your inquirer are feeling rather vulnerable at the moment.

✦ CROSS Whether upright or 'X'–shaped, a cross is one of the most powerful symbols you will find in a cup. A cross that resembles a crucifix means that your success and happiness are hard–won and well–deserved. You have overcome many obstacles to reach your goals or current favourable circumstances. Your success and accomplishments do you credit.

An 'X' shaped cross is always a warning, and should not be taken lightly. Nearby symbols will reveal whether you should beware of an individual, a career move, or other important decisions. If the 'X' is fragmented or poorly formed, it foretells obstacles and possibly losses if you undertake a project or relationship you are currently considering. If in you are doubt, don't do it.

✦ KNOTS AND TANGLES Knots and tangles symbolize anxiety and tension, usually unnecessary, but exhausting all the same. What is interfering with your progress? What is absorbing your energy by stealing your sleep or knotting your muscles? Relaxation is essential whenever you find this symbol. You will achieve much more once you are relaxed and refreshed.

✦ BUBBLES ON THE SURFACE Bubbles on the surface of your tea or coffee when it is freshly prepared signify money coming to you, but never reveal how much. You might find a forgotten $20 bill, some coins, or a mislaid cheque. Or you might win the lottery. Whatever it is that you find, positive energy is flowing in your life, however. Look for other signs of financial gain in the cup once it has been spun and drained before confidently predicting riches to your inquirer, but you can at least anticipate a good week ahead.

NUMBERS AND LETTERS

Numbers and letters should be interpreted literally, as dates, people, places, house numbers and so on. Sometimes a number refers to a period of time, such as three days or three weeks before a letter arrives or a certain event takes place.

It can be impossible to judge whether the figure refers to days, weeks, months or years. But since fortune-telling from tea or coffee cups is usually short-term – up to a year at most – years are not usually signified. Use your intuition.

DOMESTIC ANIMALS

◆ BULL *A symbol of power and endurance, suggesting supreme confidence and a rock-like determination to succeed. You must grasp opportunities, and take a firm, decisive attitude towards circumstances and events. People born under the sign of* Taurus *may also be signified, especially if the bull is accompanied by an* initial or human figure.

◆ COW *A symbol of abundance, prosperity and*

security, a cow must be interpreted along with the symbols that accompany her. For example: a cow linked with a money *symbol (the dollar or pound sign for example) suggests increased income or perhaps a little windfall. If she appears close to a* heart, *a rewarding relationship awaits you. Fertility – either creative or physical – is also suggested.*

◆ HORSE *Inner strength and a well-developed philosophy of life, carry you through most*

difficulties and crises. Often a horse signifies a journey that brings benefits in some way – perhaps a new job or successful business deal. You may need to adopt a hopeful attitude before you can benefit from current possibilities.

• DONKEY *The donkey or ass is a beast of burden, an animal that has worked tirelessly for humanity for millennia. Patience, endurance and stubborness are all suggested by this sturdy animal, meaning that you have or may need these qualities at the present time. If other symbols in the cup suggest job opportunities or a promotion you will certainly be extra-busy and perhaps even overloaded with tasks. But, like the stubborn donkey, your stamina will see you through.*

• RAM *A ram has dramatic horns, and must not be confused with a goat, which* means something different. It is the symbol for the zodiac sign Aries, and denotes assertive, dynamic energy and truly vibrant behavior. Go for it.

• SHEEP OR LAMB *Good fortune and peaceful interludes are signified generally. Specifically, the sheep counsels patience, so adopt a* 'wait-and-see' attitude to current circumstances or concerns. Assertive behavior could ruin everything at this stage. Restrain your impulses.

• GOAT *Your hard work and persistent efforts to manifest your dreams may tire you out, but you will succeed in the end. Try to relax a little, and make time for fun and* pleasure, but don't stop persevering because it will be worth it eventually. A person born under the sign of Capricorn, the goat, may be indicated – especially when an initial appears nearby.

+ **PIG** *Neither wholly good nor wholly negative, the pig denotes a mixture of jealousy and devotion. Sometimes it simply signifies greed, or a greedy individual — especially if it is accompanied by an* initial, *or other symbol suggesting someone you know.*

+ **DOG** *Loyal friends and associates will support you in everything you do, so don't be afraid to ask for help. A dog that appears to be barking or snarling represents an untrustworthy friend, who is liable to turn on you or sabotage your efforts in some way. An* initial *may appear nearby, enabling you to identify this person more accurately.*

+ **CAT** *A good-luck symbol, especially if found close to an archway or envelope sign. When next to a person or letter of the alphabet it denotes secrecy, independence, and hidden matters. You cannot control this person, any more than you can force a cat to do something it doesn't want to do. They could be quite unpredictable, and are unlikely to tell you everything you want to know. But once they trust you, you'll have a loyal friend.*

+ **RABBIT** *See also* Hare. *The rabbit is also a general symbol of increased fertility. Your business may enter a phase of growth, you may add to your family, or be bursting with bright ideas.*

WILD ANIMALS

- **DINOSAUR** *Gigantic, slow-moving creatures, dinosaurs symbolize the past, obstinate views, and maybe a need to update your life in some way. When describing someone else a dinosaur signifies old-fashioned attitudes or a fixed opinion on some important issue. This can have a negative effect on your relationship whether personal or professional. An inability to adapt or change is said to have led to the extinction of these awesome creatures. Beware, you could be stuck in the past.*

- **WHALE** *Circumstances are about to expand in your life. A whale is usually a favorable symbol, although if it is worry or irritation that are expanded it could be to the point of debilitating anxiety, particularly if you allow yourself to be swept away by negative feelings. Generally, though, this is a positive symbol. When the situation is good, it indicates that your finances, social life or your romantic prospects are about to improve.*

- **SHARK** *A shark is a clear warning against unscrupulousness, selfish people – usually one individual in particular. Such a person many seem to be charming, straightforward and honest but you will probably get an uneasy feeling when you are dealing with them. This symbol is your intuition telling you to tread carefully, even if it seems illogical or even unkind. Beware, and trust your instincts. The shark is invariably a ruthless predator.*

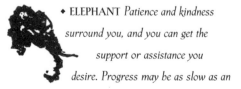

- **ELEPHANT** *Patience and kindness surround you, and you can get the support or assistance you desire. Progress may be as slow as an*

elephant ambling along, but you are certain to get there in the end. Sometimes the elephant stands for India, or matters associated with the East. Surrounding pictures will reveal whether you are about to travel.

◆ GIRAFFE *A giraffe is an exotic, magical and strange creature that is held in great respect by the Bushmen of Africa where it is believed to possess supernatural powers. A giraffe in your cup symbolizes fortuitous coincidences, and the energy or positive frame of mind needed to attract them into your life. If you maintain an open and optimistic attitude, plus a willingness to take a chance, you can create your own luck at this time. The Universe is listening.*

◆ BEAR *A bear is a powerful animal with an aggressive streak hence the saying 'like a bear with a sore head' – and may represent a grouchy, difficult person. But bears have a rich and complex symbolic history stretching back thousands of years. They are symbols of strength, courage and endurance. A she-bear with a cub denotes rebirth and renewal. Look for surrounding symbols before you decide on a meaning. A toy bear signifies childhood or children.*

◆ CAMEL *The camel is a beast of burden, and symbolizes life's burdens and pressures. You may be rather overloaded with responsibilities and commitments just now, but patience, strength and determination will help you to reach a calm oasis in the near future. You have the power to succeed.*

◆ LION *A male lion is a majestic beast, often suggesting powerful friends or influential contacts. A female lion, or lioness, promises enhanced vitality, optimism and successful family*

relationships. Either way, this is a very fortunate symbol. A lion may also symbolize an individual born under the sign of Leo if you see an initial or a face nearby in the cup.

♦ **TIGER** *Fierce, ferocious and clever,* tigers symbolize fighting for what you need or desire. But you may have to track your prey with skill and cunning tactics before you can achieve you aims. Certainly this is no time to hide behind false modesty or indecision. This could be a challenging phase, but you will be energized by your battles and stand an excellent chance of victory.

♦ **ZEBRA** *Zebras were once known as 'tiger horses', and said to be the animal sacred to* the Greek sun god Helios. In a reading they signify one of two things – adventure or travel connected with other cultures, or stubborn and wilful behavior. You must look closely at the cup to see whether the zebra represents new experiences to you or your inquirer – an arch, road or airplane might be nearby in this instance. If the zebra is close to the handle, or beside an initial or face, the second meaning applies. You, or someone close to you, are jeopardizing the stability or future of a relationship or job by refusing to explore alternative attitudes or solutions. Be more flexible.

♦ **DEER** *A gentle, shy person can be denoted by a deer. But if there are indications of work, love, or business ventures in the surrounding symbols, it is a warning against showing excessive* timidity. 'He who hesitates is lost' would be an appropriate adage for this symbol. Think carefully, and assess the tone and atmosphere of the cup. If opportunities seem clear, you must overcome your shyness and don't miss out.

• MONKEY *Monkeys counsel vigilance and caution, for someone is telling lies or deceiving you in some way. If this clever animal describes you, you are on the brink of making an unwise move or decision — especially in love. Perhaps you are deceiving yourself? Mull things over before acting on impulse.*

• WOLF *This can be interpreted in two ways, depending on what surrounds it. In a positive setting, or lightly patterned reading, the wolf indicates bravery and spiritual strength. When found amidst difficult patterns it warns of jealousy, intrigues and betrayal. Either way, it is a potent symbol, suggesting an important or challenging phase ahead.*

• KANGAROO *Kangaroos are fond of fighting, so this creature can simply suggest a rival, or argumentative friend. When close to the handle a kangaroo describes erratic energy or an inability to concentrate. You are jumping from one thing to another, and need to focus. Sometimes a kangaroo denotes Australia. Use your intuition and nearby pictures to decide what is appropriate.*

• FOX *A cunning and quick-witted individual may try to fool you or trick you in some way. In matters of love, you may have a rival or be falling for an unfaithful type. Proceed with caution.*

• HARE *There's a big difference between a hare and a rabbit, so look carefully before you identify this magical creature. A hare has long, elegant ears. If one is in your cup, something significant is brewing. A long journey may transform your life, or a relationship could begin suddenly. Be open to destiny and trust your intuition.*

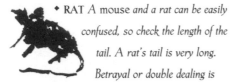

❖ RAT A mouse *and a rat can be easily confused, so check the length of the tail. A rat's tail is very long. Betrayal or double dealing is denoted, but there is a greater risk of trouble than when you see a mouse in the cup. Someone is 'a rat', so watch your step in love or business.*

❖ SQUIRREL *A hardworking person, or phase in your life. However, there may be too many different projects going on at the moment and you might be scattering your energy, just as a squirrel buries its nuts all over the place. Establish your priorities, and make some time for yourself.*

❖ TORTOISE OR TURTLE *A fortunate sign, the turtle or tortoise indicates lasting success achieved through slow and patient effort. While there may be some way to go,* like the tortoise in its race against the hare, you will get there eventually, and ultimately nothing can stop you manifesting your aims.

❖ BAT *A very busy phase is forecast in the weeks ahead, but it may be hard to make much noticeable or real progress as you flit about from one task to another, like a bat hunting insects at twilight.*

❖ MOUSE *Be meticulous in your financial and business dealings, and check all the details very carefully. A mouse or mice may denote minor irritations, or even major problems with cash, credit and business arrangements. The possibility of a swindle or scam is high at the moment. Be cautious and scrutinize all documents that come your way very carefully over the time period indicated by its position in the cup.*

◆ ALLIGATOR OR CROCODILE *A ruthless opponent or implacable enemy lurks somewhere in your life, usually in your professional life. This individual may outwardly feign cordiality and friendship; so be wary and keep your own counsel.*

◆ SNAKE *Perhaps one of the most complex and fascinating symbols of all, the snake has evoked a mixture of awe, revulsion and worship for millennia. Your first step is to decide whether this is a serpent, or simply the initial 'S'. Sometimes there will be more than one set of undulating curves, then your task is simple. Otherwise, consider carefully the snake's shape and position in the cup to determine your interpretation:*

A COILED SNAKE is a warning sign. You may have a wily enemy whose negative intentions are masked behind a show of friendship or apparent good will. You may be in a vulnerable state, so take care of your valuables and be wary of others. This is a bad time to sign contracts or enter binding commitments.

An UNCOILED SNAKE (in a line) symbolizes wisdom, renewal, and the ability to make very important decisions about your future. A decision of some kind is indicated too. If the snake is seen at the rim of the cup the decision is imminent. Further down, there is some way to go.

◆ LIZARD *What are you worrying about? There is no need for anxiety, so relax. Your fears are groundless, as you will soon realize. Meanwhile, you would be wise to find something to take your mind off your troubles. They are largely imaginary.*

◆ FROG *Fertility and abundance are about to enter your life when this ancient good-luck symbol appears.*

Your creativity overflows and your love life is poised to enter a joyful phase. Sometimes this foretells a pregnancy, especially in a woman's cup. Generally, though, it denotes the fairytale handsome prince, disguised as a good friend or unlikely love object. Try a kiss, and see what happens!

 • FISH Wisdom and knowledge are the key attributes of this symbol. You may be in a position to teach someone, or learn something valuable yourself. Intuitive gifts or feelings are emphasized; pay attention to your dreams and waking 'flashes'. If placed beside a heart or flowers, the fish symbolizes fertility and passion.

It can represent someone born under the zodiac sign Pisces, whose symbol is two fish, swimming in opposite directions.

 • CRAB The crab traditionally approaches everything sideways on, symbolizing an inability to be direct in its dealings with others. Does this apply to you? It is a defensive creature, although once it grips on to something with its claws it is tenacious and never lets go. Perhaps you are holding on to your past in some areas of your life and you really should let go? Usually there is an emotional reason for this, plus a fear of the future, and change and what they might bring. You may not be ready to move forward just yet, but try thinking about it or discussing possibilities with friends. They may be able to shed some light on something that is holding you back.

A crab can also symbolize someone born under the zodiac sign of Cancer, especially if it is found near an initial or a human figure.

BIRDS

• **BIRDS** (general) A single bird means news and messages. If it appears to be standing or perching, there could be a delay. A flying bird means good news, so look carefully at surrounding symbols to see what form this might take.

A flock of flying birds denotes great excitement, and increases the amount of news you will receive.

Sometimes birds symbolize travel or journeys, especially when beside a road symbol.

• **GOOSE** Your project or venture will be a great success, and likely to make money for you. Generally, a symbol of happiness and prosperity.

• **PEACOCK** A dual symbol, meaning pride and display. Also denotes beauty, fortune and marriage or serious courtship. Look for other signs of romance, such as a heart, when using the second interpretation.

This is generally a lucky sign, but remain wary for the time being and don't make snap decisions or hasty commitments at the moment.

• **EAGLE** A complex symbol of power and transcendence, the eagle soars effortlessly through the air, signifying ambition and high expectations. Sometimes it symbolizes the United States of America, especially if the picture looks heraldic. It is a fortune sign, usually indicating future success and achievement.

• **CROW, RAVEN OR ROOK** Traditionally birds of ill omen, these birds represent worries and tension, and are a warning to take it easy. You are undermining your health through stress.

◆ **PARROT** *Although clever birds, parrots are nonetheless a warning sign against thoughtless gossip. Do not pass on information to others at this time, since it could backfire. A garrulous friend can also be denoted. Be discreet, and all will be well.*

◆ **HENS AND CHICKENS** *Domestic delights and the comforts of childhood offer you happiness now. Perhaps you'll be spending time with family or meet up with a lifelong friend. Overall, home life is very sweet when these birds appear.*

◆ **DOVE** *A universal symbol of peace and love, doves once symbolized Aphrodite or Venus, the goddess of love and beauty. As messenger birds, doves invariably bring news of a loved one and affectionate communications of every kind. An extremely uplifting and fortunate symbol to find in any reading.*

◆ **OWL** *A bird of the night, owls are associated with mystery, magic and the supernatural on the one hand and with wisdom, knowledge and learning on the other. Connect these meanings and you can see that the owl denotes an interest in studying the secrets of the paranormal, divination or alternative philosophies and mystic arts. Or you could simply embark on a course of study, acquire new skills, or immerse yourself in learning a language. When surrounded by difficult or negative symbols the owl warns of betrayal and deception, especially in love. But only accept this meaning if other symbols support it.*

◆ **ROOSTER** *The rooster's piercing cry acts as a wake-up call, and announces this colorful bird's presence in no uncertain terms. A rooster can denote an extrovert, confident, and even slightly boastful individual when linked to an initial, face or body shape. 'Here I am, notice me!' When not describing*

you or another person, it urges you to seize the moment and make a start on that project you have been thinking about. Wake up!

• SWAN *Graceful and beautiful, swans have a long history as romantic symbols of enduring love and lasting marriage. There are many fairy tales and myths which link the swan with both love and music; it is a delightful and fortunate symbol to find in any reading. If you are interested in a relationship question you can relax and anticipate a lasting union with a faithful and devoted partner.*

• VULTURE *A vulture is a powerful bird with great survival instincts which has been respected and even revered in numerous ancient cultures. But because it feeds on carrions, it is also a bird with negative connotations symbolizing enemies, difficulties and unpleasant people in general. Be discreet now,*

and keep your hopes and dreams strictly confidential. Someone may be planning to benefit from your ideas, or steal your job or lover away from you.

• SWALLOW *Every summer swallows, swifts and housemartins migrate from the south to Europe, flying south again as the autumn begins. Swallows are symbols of new beginnings, hope and good luck – especially if you are planning a journey far-away places. Swallows are also associated with the goddess of love, Venus or Aphrodite, and can signify a new romance or special love affair.*

• NEST *A nest is a sweet symbol of emotional security and the desire to create a safe and loving home, relationship or lifestyle. If you have none of these yet you will soon find a way to acquire them. A committed relationship is often signified by this symbol, especially if it is accompanied by signs of romance.*

INSECTS

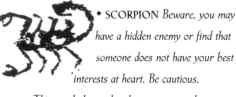

◆ BUTTERFLY *An ancient symbol of the soul, butterflies denote pleasure and passing joys. Occasionally they are a warning against fickle actions or an inability to settle down to a task or relationship. Usually though, they suggest delightful experiences and are considered lucky.*

◆ SCORPION *Beware, you may have a hidden enemy or find that someone does not have your best interests at heart. Be cautious. This symbol can also denote someone born under the sign of* Scorpio.

◆ SNAIL *Either a warning to slow down, or an indication of slow progress in a project, love affair or events in general. But snails are generally regarded as lucky*

symbols, so the end result will be pleasing. Just cultivate patience, and remember the adage 'more haste, less speed'. Eventually, you will succeed.

◆ BEETLE *Revered in ancient Egypt as a symbol of renewal, beetles are fortunate, vital symbols of progress and developments. However, if you find this sign near negative indications, it can denote lack of foresight or a limited perspective. Seek advice.*

◆ BUGS *A number of distractions or worries destroy your peace of mind. But try to gain a sense of perspective, and you'll see that minor annoyances have simply spiralled out of control and assumed a significance they do not deserve. Define your priorities, relax, and you'll achieve a lot more. Stress undermines your progress if you let it.*

• SPIDER *Traditionally signifies money luck, although you are unlikely to win thousands or discover priceless treasure in your attic. A small win, promotion, or gift of money can be confidently expected in the near future.*

• SPIDER'S WEB *A supremely potent symbol, the spider's web is a sign of creative power and the forces of destiny or fate. A spider's web can also suggest plots and schemes, or traps and trickery. Look closely at surrounding symbols to decide on a positive or negative interpretation. Either way, fate is at work and you are entering a significant period in your life.*

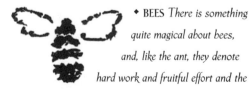

• BEES *There is something quite magical about bees, and, like the ant, they denote hard work and fruitful effort and the* rewards that accompany them. Bees sometimes bring messages, so look closely at surrounding symbols to see if this is so.

• ANT *Hard work lies ahead, for you are entering a busy phase. The results of your efforts should please you, since the ant is a famously productive and well-organized creature.*

• GRASSHOPPER *The song of these insects instantly conjures up the spirit of summer nights; and symbolizes the warmth and expansion traditionally associated with this fertile season. Enjoy a positive time, but do not forget to make some plans for the future too. The grasshopper is also associated with fickle energies and a restless mind that cannot concentrate on anything for long. Remember that neither the balmy summer nor grasshoppers last forever.*

NATURAL PHENOMENA

♦ SUN Look closely; a circle with rays or dots surrounding it should be interpreted as the Sun, otherwise it is just a circle. The Sun is a very special sign to find in a cup, symbolizing life, success and happiness. Sometimes it signifies a hot country, especially when combined with signs that relate to travel. It can also mean summertime, particularly when found at the bottom of the cup during spring. In this case, look to see what pictures are nearby for clues about an important event during the summer. The Sun is an extremely fortunate and vibrant symbol, suggesting a bright future.

♦ MOON Again, look closely. Is it a Full Moon or a circle? Only your intuition can be your guide here, so go with your first impressions.

If it is a FULL MOON, you or your inquirer are in a particularly emotional frame of mind and may be feeling restless or ultra sensitive.

A CRESCENT MOON means changes. What kind of change, and when, will be revealed by pictures nearby and the position in the cup. A crescent Moon with a house, for example, indicates a move or important domestic changes. With an initial, or sign indicating a person, it means an important or meaningful meeting with someone who could bring about lasting change in your life.

♦ STARS Stars can be shown in various ways. But however they appear, they bring a little magic into any reading. The phrase 'wish upon a star' is appropriate here, since this lovely symbol means that a wish will come true if you have the courage to dream and the desire to enrich your life.

A star can also mean recognition and success,

either for you or someone close to you. Either way, this is a positive and lucky symbol. Any challenges in the reading will be overcome.

◆ CLOUDS *What kind of clouds do you see? Small fluffy ones mean that you're elated and optimistic about something or someone. Practical questions and considerations come later. For the moment enjoy feeling so good. Thick, dark clouds are another matter, suggesting problems and an inability to be objective about them. However, like real clouds, these difficulties will soon pass, so don't be downhearted.*

◆ RAINDROPS OR TEARDROPS *This symbol looks the same, whether you think it looks like rain or tears. Either way, sadness and a release from bottled-up feelings is suggested. It's time to be more open with yourself and those you love and care for.*

◆ LIGHTNING *An exciting, yet unsettling sign meaning inspiration, intuition, and startling insights. It can also portend sudden events that alter the course of your life or plans, such as falling in love, or waking up one day and deciding to travel the world. Life will not be dull when this symbol appears.*

◆ RAINBOW *Similar to an arch, the rainbow is wider and more gently curved. It is a basic luck symbol, meaning prosperity and good fortune. If you have a secret desire, or were wishing for something when you spun your cup you can anticipate your wish coming true.*

◆ TORNADO OR WHIRLWIND *Stormy weather is forecast, so prepare for a turbulent and unsettling phase. You may not be able to control events, indeed, flexibility is essential now if you want to avoid stress. This is the ultimate* 'wind of change', blowing at gale force. Challenging though it seems, a positive outcome is likely, so don't resist this challenge.

• FIRE *Fire represents passion, sexual longing, anger and all the 'hot' emotions that threaten to engulf you. To discover what is fuelling the flames look to see what lurks nearby. Are you aflame with desire or burning with rage and ambition? If you are reading for yourself you will already know the answer. If reading for another, proceed gently. Intense feelings are close to the surface.*

• COMET *A comet is an amazing, awe-inspiring sight for anyone lucky enough to be in the right place at the right time to see it. Ancient astrologers associated comets with major change and dramatic events, which is more or less how you should interpret this symbol when you find one in your cup. You are approaching an important point in your life, a truly fateful and pivotal moment when your dreams become real and your hopes for the future stand every chance of fulfilment. Do not hold back or hesitate on the brink, at this time wishes can really come true.*

LANDSCAPES

◆ ISLAND *An island can be interpreted literally, as an actual location. Accompanying symbols usually affirm this, for example something that is associated with the place such as palm trees, a particular* musical instrument, *a religious monument, or even an* initial. *If none of this makes sense, you can interpret it as a symbol of defensiveness, isolation, or simple loneliness. The rest of the cup is likely to support this meaning, especially when someone is unhappy or coping with a new neighborhood, job, or recent relationship breakdown.*

◆ MOUNTAINS *These can be interpreted in two separate ways. Firstly, a mountainous place could be important – a trip, someone who lives there, a job and so on will all be revealed by accompanying* symbols, or initials. *Otherwise, a mountain represents a major ambition, usually requiring long-term commitment, energy and determination in order to reach your goal.*

◆ VOLCANO *Expect eruptions in your personal life when a volcano appears. A situation that has been building up for a long time is no longer acceptable, and some kind of confrontation is necessary to clear the air. This may refer to you, or someone close to you, at home or at work. But an unpleasant episode will help to release everyone, and you'll be able to make a fresh start.*

◆ HILLS *A gentle challenge lies ahead, but overcoming it will bring both pleasure, wisdom, and an enduring sense of achievement.*

◆ VALLEY *A valley naturally occurs between two hills or mountains, and is only significant if clearly formed. Like its accompanying symbols it denotes challenges and heartfelt goals and further increases your chances of success and satisfaction.*

 ◆ RIVERS *Rivers, streams, and* wavy lines *all look the same in a cup and all indicate emotional episodes where your feelings are very close to the surface. What kind of feelings will be shown by the look of the cup in general, and nearby symbols in particular. A number of wavy lines together suggests the sea, intensifying the emotional atmosphere of the reading.*

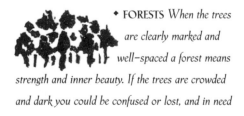 ◆ FORESTS *When the trees are clearly marked and well-spaced a forest means strength and inner beauty. If the trees are crowded and dark you could be confused or lost, and in need of guidance and clarity. Making decisions would be unwise just now, try to gain some perspective. Perhaps a walk in a real forest might do the trick?*

 ◆ ROADS *Roads and* lines *are interchangeable symbols, meaning journeys. Generally, the clearer and straighter they are the more successful and straightforward the trip will be. Breaks suggest delays or diversions.*

◆ ROCKS *Rocks are basically lumpy gatherings of tea leaves or coffee grounds, suggesting that energy is not flowing freely in some area of your life. There are obstacles to be overcome; someone or something is blocking your progress. Think about circumstances or people that make you feel tired or dispirited; and you will soon identify the culprit and smooth your path. By confronting the problem, you will be able to move ahead.*

TREES AND FLOWERS

◆ FLOWERS *Generally a lucky, happy symbol indicating success, praise and compliments. If you see an* initial *or human shape next to them you'll be receiving some flowers very soon, especially if the flowers form a* bouquet.

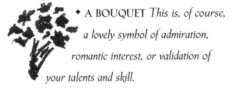

◆ A BOUQUET *This is, of course, a lovely symbol of admiration, romantic interest, or validation of your talents and skill.*

◆ A SINGLE FLOWER *This shape is even more heartfelt than a bouquet, and suggests love or generous and genuine appreciation of your gifts. It is the most potent symbol amongst this charming and uplifting little group.*

Look for nearby symbols, such as a heart, *to see what form this admiration takes.*

◆ DAISY *A daisy, once poetically known as 'the eye of the day', signifies innocence, the morning, and often the beginning of something new and fresh. Above all, it denotes a bright and happy phase.*

◆ LILY OR FLEUR DE LYS *A very feminine symbol, the lily is especially fortunate in a woman's cup, for it is associated with the Greek goddess of love, Aphrodite, and the goddess Hera, who presided over marriage. The lily is inextricably linked with female power and fertility. It means good health, serenity, and a receptive state of mind. In a man's cup it can signify a new woman, although other indications of romance must be present to confirm this. Generally, a loving atmosphere surrounds you and you can look forward to joy very soon.*

♦ **ROSE** *An almost universal symbol of romantic love and admiration, the rose signifies either a new romance or the deepening of an existing relationship – perhaps a commitment or declaration of someone's true feelings. Roses, like lilies, are associated with the love goddesses of many ancient mythologies, and the power of these beliefs has remained alive throughout the centuries. Whatever transpires, your heart is beginning to open and you are in the right frame of mind to receive love, passion, joy and abundance.*

♦ **LEAF** *Leaves are connected with the passage of time, hence the saying 'turning over a new leaf', since leaves also refer to pages in a book. Springtime, new growth and fresh starts are possible now. A cycle of events is just beginning or coming to a close, either way the changes involved will be natural and inevitable – just like the growth and decay of leaves themselves.*

♦ **BUSHES AND SHRUBS** *Neither good nor bad, bushes represent hidden information, and concealed facts. Perhaps you are the one who is deliberately holding something back? Or, you may not possess all the facts about a new job, potential partner in love or business, or speculative venture. There is nothing sinister about bushes, but do not make hasty decisions just now. You need more information.*

♦ **TREES** *A tree standing by itself in your cup is an ancient symbol of life in myriad mythologies, and often refers to your roots, family, and heritage in general.*

Family matters will invariably be important during the time period indicated by the position of the tree, and any accompanying symbols nearby.

A stark, **LEAFLESS WINTER TREE** *may denote difficulties or family problems – perhaps with your parents, or siblings or children.*

A **TREE WITH LEAVES** *is a very fortunate sign of health and prosperity for you and the ones around you that you love.*

A **GROUP OF TREES** *multiplies the positive benefits suggested by one healthy tree. If linked with any travel symbols it denotes a visit to the countryside. If there is a* bird, *you will receive news from some distance – usually good news.*

EVERGREEN TREES *symbolize enduring relationships or business involvements, also prosperity.*

♦ **PALM TREE** *Wealth and security generally, although be meticulous when interpreting this symbol to mean a tropical location or even a holiday. As ever, context is all-important – are you reading the cup in a cold, wintry city or are you sitting on a palm-fringed beach? Do you or your inquirer have connections with tropical countries – either in love, family or business? Flex your creative muscles and allow intuition to guide your reading.*

♦ **IVY** *Faith and endurance are required, but friends will help you to succeed, so don't be too independent. This is a good time to gain support for your endeavors, so remember that if you don't ask, the answer will always be no.*

BUILDINGS

♦ HOUSE *In most cases a house refers to your home life, and can indicate a move of home. Home life will be important during the coming weeks, and should bring you happiness and security. Any challenging symbols nearby reveal difficulties at home, or a troubled home life. Generally, however, the sign of a house is positive and reassuring.*

♦ CHURCH OR PLACE OF WORSHIP *Spiritual enlightenment and protection are suggested, whether or not you practise your religion in a formal way. These are potent and powerful symbols, indicating a special time in your life. If you are experiencing difficulties at this time, you will find comfort and inspiration in quiet contemplation. Traditionally, no negative symbols can reduce the power for good represented here.*

♦ LIGHTHOUSE OR BEACON *You can help and inspire others and may find yourself in a position of authority or leadership in the near future.*

♦ WINDMILL *There are many ideas or influences around you, and you may not be ready to make a clear-cut decision. Speculative ventures should go well, but only if your heart is in them. Where you have genuine doubts, listen to your inner voice and wait until you feel certain. Further developments are likely, so wait and see where the wind blows.*

♦ CASTLE *You may be limiting yourself in some way, or playing safe. While self-protection and sensible security precautions are necessary there may*

48

be too much emphasis on boundaries and not enough adventure or experimentation in your life. Step outside your castle and expand your horizons a little. You could be pleasantly surprised by what you see.

✦ **PYRAMID** *What immediately sprang to mind when you first looked at this symbol? Did you think − 'a pyramid', or did you just see a* triangle? *Go with your intuition, and interpret accordingly. If you saw a pyramid it can be interpreted as ambition leading to the pinnacle of success and triumph. Obviously, it could also mean Ancient Egypt, but only if this is particularly relevant to you and your interests.*

✦ **OBELISK** *Another architectural form from the ancient world, but unmistakable this time. An obelisk means that you must accomplish some important task or journey alone, no one can help you and indeed, you may not want them*

to. *You will be successful, but prepare to meet this challenge and keep your spirits up. Your achievements will be hard−won, well−deserved and of lasting value in your life.*

✦ **WALL** *There is some kind of barrier between you and your goals, or you and someone else. Perhaps there is a misunderstanding between you, or some difference of opinion that threatens your relationship. Do not allow this to continue, since you are likely to regret it. Walls can be overcome, but you need to act quickly.*

✦ **BRIDGE** *A bridge always leads to something or someone, and can represent a decision or a change of circumstances. It is an important symbol of movement in your life, so look carefully at nearby pictures to discover the precise nature of coming events. They could be life−changing.*

◆ **DOOR** *A door can look very similar to an arch, and in fact has much the same interpretation, although doors usually refer to a wider range of opportunities or new possibilities. An open door invites you to step through into a new chapter in your life, usually one you've been striving for. This is a hopeful and positive symbol to find in any reading.*

◆ **STAIRS OR STEPS** *You are about to be promoted, or receive news of a successful conclusion to a project. General success is also suggested, whatever your field of endeavor. You will soon be in a position to celebrate.*

◆ **WINDOW** *Opportunities in general, but an enhanced imagination in particular, is forecast when a window appears in a reading. You will be in an inventive, intuitive frame of mind so make a note of any ideas or desires. This is a good time to develop artistic skills, solve problems, or learn more about your unconscious mind and psychic abilities. Invest a little effort, and you will soon reap big rewards.*

◆ **ARCH** *An arch is always an opportunity or opening, usually involving money or travel. It is positive and exciting, so look at nearby symbols to decide what kind of possibilities are on offer.*

◆ **FENCE** *Unfortunately, this is not a very positive symbol, for a fence reveals limitations and restrictions. You are 'fenced in' in some way – either personally or professionally – and could be feeling trapped or frustrated by circumstances. You might also be unable to make a decision because you are hard to please or find it difficult to make decisions in general. What is stopping you? Once you can identify your misgivings you will be able to do something to change or overcome them.*

DOMESTIC OBJECTS

 ◆ CANDLE *A candle is invariably a hopeful symbol, meaning that there is enough light to see your way, even if circumstances seem difficult at the moment. Inner light or clarity also offers you help and guidance now. Your higher-self or guardian angel can illuminate your path. You only have to ask for help.*

◆ KEY *Your life is about to take a turn for the better when a key appears in the cup. Success, happy relationships and increased status are likely – perhaps not all at once, but nearby symbols should reveal which area of your life is specifically affected.*

◆ COMB *A new hairstyle or even a whole new wardrobe could be the answer to your question right now. But under most circumstances, a new image would work wonders, so plan some personal changes and improve your appearance in some way. Your increased self-confidence will attract positive events into your life.*

◆ BRUSH *Is this a hairbrush, a household brush, or a paintbrush? All brushes signify the need for improvements, decorating or just a clearout. Personal renovations are necessary when you see a hairbrush, while your environment needs smartening up when you find a domestic or paintbrush. Some serious spring-cleaning will help you to change your luck for the better.*

 ◆ BROOM *A broom symbolizes a new home. If this seems unlikely, a broom sweeps away the past, and heralds a brand new era in your life. Either way, you can regard this as an energizing and optimistic symbol of practical changes to come.*

◆ SCISSORS *Scissors always cut something, and can denote the end of a job, relationship, or friendship. A separation from something or someone is likely now. It may not be your choice, but with ties cut, you will be free to move on into the next chapter of your life. So do not be disheartened by this rather uncompromising symbol.*

◆ UMBRELLA OR PARASOL *The essence of this symbol is protection from harm, loss, or risk — usually financial or practical matters, but occasionally romantic situations.*

◆ LAMP *Insight and guidance are available to you now. You may be in a position to help someone else, or be offered valuable help when you most need it. Either way, you can expect some light to fall on anything that has been puzzling you.*

◆ LADDER *You are climbing the ladder of success, and must not give up now. Ancient myths and legends are full of stories about magical ladders, all symbolizing spiritual progress and increasing wisdom. You may need some encouragement, so here it is. You will reach your dreams and manifest your heart's desire if you keep going. Don't look down.*

◆ VASE *There are secrets in your life — usually of a romantic nature. You may have a secret admirer, or be unable to declare your true feelings to someone special. Whatever the nature of the secret, it is about to be revealed, but beware, as harm could result.*

◆ BOTTLE *An explosive atmosphere prevails, so be careful. Overdoing it is likely; so eat, drink and be merry, but put the brakes on when you know you should, or your party mood will be replaced by regret and remorse.*

◆ CUP *Adopt a relaxed and patient attitude, and do not be assertive or demanding if you wish* to avoid criticism from others. While you may indeed want and deserve more, this is not the right time to say so. Others could be in an oversensitive mood, and it would be better to bide your time.

 ◆ PLATE *A plate should be interpreted as a circle unless you see something on it, such as fruit or bread.* In this case, you will receive an invitation to a social event that could yield some interesting contacts.

 ◆ DISH OR BOWL *Dishes and bowls always contain something* pleasant – invitations, money, or generosity from friends, family or lovers. Nearby symbols, such as a bow or a box, often offer clues, but in general you can expect some enjoyable experiences and probably a good meal as well.

◆ JUG *Your friends are planning a celebration or party, or you will shortly be enjoying a happy occasion with kindred spirits.* An air of generosity and uplifting events accompanies the jug which is always – symbolically – full of something delicious and refreshing, or waiting to be filled with a cool drink or some other tasty liquid.

◆ KNIFE *This symbol is a warning against sharp words, negative thinking, or risky ventures. It may signify you, in which case watch what* you say and count to ten before making that 'cutting' remark or amusing comment at someone else's expense. When the knife signifies someone in your life – perhaps there is an initial or a face close by – this person is not to be trusted with your most intimate secrets or tender feelings. You will be wounded if you are too trusting or naive. Be on your guard. Time will reveal all.

• FORK *Circumstances may be tricky, but you have loyal friends and will receive the help, support or advice you need. Do not hesitate to ask.*

• SPOON *Someone is stirring up trouble for you, either by spreading gossip or perhaps by taking active steps to block your progress or interfere in your private life. Keep your own counsel and only confide in those you trust completely.*

• HAMMER *A hammer signifies energy and determination to get your point of view across, literally hammering your point home. Sometimes this symbolizes someone who is trying to convince you that they are right or persuade you to agree to some plan or project of theirs. Such a person may not know when to stop promoting themselves, but generally this is a positive symbol of constructive action.*

• HOOK *Are you hooked on someone or something? What has captured your imagination? We either hang something from a hook to keep it in place, or use a hook to catch a fish. You are either caught in a situation you find hard to escape from, or you are aiming to be the one who catches a new job, lover or other prize. Nearby symbols will reveal more information.*

• BASKET *Baskets are used for carrying things, and so symbolize increase on one level or another. Sometimes this means that you will be welcoming a new pet or a new baby into your life soon. Mostly a basket denotes harvest, abundance and material gain.*

• KETTLE *A symbol closely linked with your domestic life, a kettle foretells much activity and visitors at home. You can expect a guest or guests in the near a future, and can look forward to an entertaining visit.*

◆ TEAPOT OR COFFEE POT
A special visitor is coming to
see you, but this is unlikely to have
romantic implications. A teapot or coffee pot signifies
social get–togethers with friends, one of whom is
very much in tune with you now. A rewarding and
inspiring friendship is about to begin, or an existing
connection will deepen.

◆ AXE You have the courage
and determination to overcome obstacles,
and literally cut down opposition to your wishes,
ideas or plans. There is much power and energy
associated with this symbol so make sure you use this
phase to make outstanding and rapid progress.

◆ BARREL OR CASK A barrel is
intended to contain something and is
therefore a symbol of abundance and
sufficient supplies for your needs. This
could be your finances, but is more likely to refer
to friendship, fun and laughter. If the barrel is
surrounded by symbols of difficulty or lack you might
be 'scraping the bottom of the barrel' in search of
enough cash, or enough emotional fulfilment. It could
be a time when you feel restricted in some way. For
example, if there is a fence nearby, you could be
restricting yourself by refusing to consider other
options. A knife or scorpion would suggest
someone blocking your path. Look carefully, a
remedy will soon suggest itself; the rest is up to you.

FURNITURE

◆ **CHAIR** *Someone is coming into your life, either an addition to your family or as an important new friend or romantic involvement.*

◆ **TABLE** *Rewards are in store when you find a table in your cup. You may be the generous one, as you find yourself in a position to help others who have supported you. Or, you may receive a lovely gift or some other favor from someone who appreciates your efforts on their behalf. Either way, this is positive and indicates a happy interlude.*

◆ **BED** *A decision to form a close connection with someone, emotionally or professionally, must be approached with care and caution. If you have any doubts do not act hastily, but heed the advice of this symbol and 'sleep on it'. Your dreams or waking thoughts will guide you towards the right path.*

◆ **CUSHIONS OR PILLOWS** *Be very certain you are not looking at a square or rectangle, since the interpretation differs. Interpret your first thought, and if you see cushions proceed accordingly. Cushions mean comfort and protection, but can also indicate laziness and poor motivation. If you can see opportunities in this cup, the cushions warn against a negative approach or procrastination.*

◆ **RUGS OR CARPETS** *Look for patterns, fringes, and other indications that this is a carpet and not a square or rectangle. Again, go with your first thought and trust your intuition. A rug or carpet signifies happy social events and genuine friendships.*

FOOD

‣ FRUIT (*general*) A productive phase lies ahead, particularly in your emotional life. Although fruit does not suggest romance, it does indicate improvement in your social life, family links, and perhaps relationships with work mates too. A happy and balanced life generates positive energy and attracts good experiences, so this symbol is also one of general optimism and success.

‣ APPLE A symbol of life and creativity, the apple can simply mean vitality and good health or signify an upturn in inventive, creative thinking. If you are an artist of any kind this is a particularly resonant symbol for you.

‣ PEAR Success and improvements in general can be expected when you find this fruit depicted in your cup. Victorian readers associated pears with social success and popularity, often achieved through a relationship or marriage to a dynamic or wealthy partner.

‣ GRAPES Grapes signify abundance. Whether this relates to financial affairs, love or health should be revealed by nearby pictures. Even if you can't be precise, it is safe to say that this is an uplifting sign.

‣ LEMONS Something is sour or bitter, perhaps your emotions or perhaps the feelings of another towards you. This is not a happy symbol, but the unpleasant feelings it reveals are about to change. Life can be sweet, change your attitude or put some distance between you and the negative person indicated by the lemon. As the saying goes, 'If life hands you lemons, make lemonade'.

◆ VEGETABLES *Prosperity and nourishment are forecast, especially if you have been working on any long-term projects or schemes. It is time to reap your harvest and take pleasure in your achievements.*

 ◆ EGGS *Is the egg whole, or is it cracked and broken? If whole, the egg is a beautiful symbol of new life, new beginnings and certain success. If cracked or broken it indicates financial problems, failed plans or difficulties getting things moving in the right direction. But the egg is a positive symbol, and even if broken, you can take steps towards setting things straight. All is not lost, so pick up the pieces and try again.*

◆ LOAF OF BREAD *A basic food, bread means nourishment and well-being will be important topics in the near future. Are you looking after yourself properly?*

Basic health care is one clear meaning of this symbol, but what about your spiritual and emotional life? At some level you need food — so ponder this symbol and you'll arrive at an answer.

◆ CAKE *A celebration, a wish fulfilled, or even a dream-come-true is indicated by this symbol of welcome and special occasions. Sometimes it signifies a party or anniversary. Generally, you can interpret some good luck and a reason to smile. A symbol of happiness.*

◆ MUSHROOM *If you think about the way mushrooms suddenly appear as if from nowhere, you will see why they symbolize abundance and fertility of every kind. This may indicate a pregnancy or foretell an especially creative period in your life. You could be bursting with ideas, or about to begin a business that will be very successful and grow as rapidly as a field full of multiplying mushrooms.*

THE BODY

◆ **HEAD OR FACE** *If there is an initial nearby this symbol refers to someone you already know or are about to meet. If close to the rim or the handle it warns against too much thinking, analysis, or inner debate. If the head or face is seen in profile, look in the direction of its gaze to see what is causing the problem.*

◆ **EYE** *A universal symbol of protection against enemies dating back to Ancient Egypt, the eye is a powerful symbol to find in any readings. It can suggest something simple, like increased charm and personal attractiveness, or it can signify a particularly intuitive phase. It is a lucky sign, so don't waste your time procrastinating. You can make fulfilling progress now if you are prepared to take a chance and trust in your forthcoming good fortune.*

◆ **EAR** *An ear means you will soon hear something to your advantage, usually in person or by telephone but sometimes via other methods of communication. It always represents positive news and cannot be diminished by negative symbols. Likely subjects will be found near.*

◆ **MOUTH** *A pair of lips on their own usually mean a new romance is about to enter your life. Look for other signs, such as a heart, to see whether this is a major connection or just a passing flirtation with a hot date.*

◆ **NOSE** *Secrets are waiting to be 'sniffed out' when you see this sign. These may be personal, or refer to buried ideas and inspirations of a creative or money spinning nature. Make time to listen to you intuition for dynamic results.*

* HAND *Where is the hand pointing? What you find there is very meaningful and affects the entire reading. When the hand is flat it represents the hand of karma or destiny, and is both fortunate and protective. Life is about to take an interesting, and possibly fateful, turn for the better.*

* FOOT *You will be 'putting your best foot forward' and moving on in your life. This is a dynamic symbol promising significant movement and interesting developments in your career, love life, or even the location of your home or workplace.*

* BABY *The clearest symbol of new life, a baby is usually read literally as a forthcoming birth or pregnancy for you or someone close to you. Occasionally, a baby refers to a new life in another way – perhaps a treasured project or creative goal is* about to take off. Mostly, however, a baby should be interpreted as an infant. If pregnancy is not desired, make sure you are extra vigilant!*

* ARM *When you find an arm in the cup you must look to see where it is pointing. An arm pointing upwards means new directions, often spiritually or creatively. A horizontal arm means support and help will be available to you, or you could be in a position to offer these to someone else. An arm pointing downwards can indicate mild depression, lack of energy or sufficient willpower to motivate yourself. Perhaps you need a new health regime, a weekend break or some positive thinking in your life?*

* LEG *Unless someone close to you is experiencing a problem with their legs, you should interpret this in the same way as a foot; a symbol of movement, progress and new developments.*

TRANSPORTATION

 ✦ CAR *When a car is clearly drawn it signifies a trip. If* you see straight lines *nearby, it will be a long journey, either for a long weekend or a holiday. Otherwise, you will just be travelling a little further than usual, perhaps to a neighboring town or outlying district. A poorly formed car symbol forwarns you about mechanical problems. It could be time to take your car for an overhaul.*

When an initial *accompanies the car it denotes a visit from someone identified by this letter.*

✦ TRAIN *Steady progess towards your goals is now possible. There may be stops along the way, but ultimately nothing can stop you reaching your chosen destination. If other signs, such as* buildings or palm trees *agree, the train represents a real journey. To discover when, look at this symbol's position.*

✦ AIRPLANE *A long trip is coming up, and your destination should be revealed by surrounding symbols such as a* letter, a palm tree *or a* building. *The trip itself might only last for a few days, but you will be travelling a great distance.*

 ✦ BOAT *This is a delightful, lucky symbol to find in your cup, for a boat symbolizes that your ship is about to come in to harbour. What will it bring? Some fortune–tellers suggest visitors, others romance or financial luck. It is safe to say that life is about to take a turn for the better; look at nearby symbols to see what form this lucky break will take.*

 ✦ BICYCLE *The wonderful thing about a bicycle is that you control the pace, and can move*

freely while a larger vehicle gets stuck or restricted. A bicycle means you take an individual approach to life, perhaps even an eccentric one. Certainly your aims and ambitions are original and possibly unique. But your direction will bring you success and happiness, so keep following your chosen path.

♦ WHEEL *A powerful symbol of unimaginable antiquity, the wheel is a sign of inevitable change, invariably for the better. This is the ancient Wheel of Fortune, which turns by itself and cannot be controlled by human willpower, wishes or desires. It is also inextricably linked with the concept of time's unfolding patterns. Your life is about to evolve in a new direction, perhaps one you had not previously considered. You may meet someone who will affect your life in some important way — through love or in your career. Events outside your control will create opportunities, change and ultimately progress. You could feel pleasantly confused or even out of control, but go with the flow and allow events to reveal themselves to you at their own pace.*

MISCELLANEOUS SYMBOLS

◆ HEART *A perfect heart shape in your cup signifies love and romance, just as you would expect. But any breaks or lines inside the symbol mean heartache or painful relationships. A very faint heart shape composed of tiny dots foretells an important love affair some distance into the future, wherever you see it. Is there a face or an initial close by? If not, you will just have to contain your curiosity and wait. Someone special is on his or her way.*

◆ BELLS *Bells bring good news, often relating to love and marriage, but sometimes heralding a promotion, salary rise, or other pleasing event.*

◆ CROWN *Success, honor and recognition of your talents and abilities lie ahead. What form this will*

take should be indicated by symbols appearing nearby in the cup. Generally, this is a very positive and reassuring sign.

◆ ANCHOR *A clearly-defined anchor is a lucky symbol, meaning success and stability in love or business. A weak-looking or faint anchor suggests instability and changeable conditions in your life. Perhaps your relationships are difficult, a love affair is not going well, and your working life is difficult. Maybe it is time for you to sail away to a new stretch of water?*

◆ CHAIN *A well-formed chain means a serious commitment or undertaking that will be good for you is imminent. The events leading up to this could have been largely outside your control, so you will* probably feel a sense of fate or destiny at work. A broken chain means trouble, disruption and unsettled conditions now, or in the time ahead.

• BOW A happy and fortunate symbol, a bow means a gift or celebration in the near future, often associated with anniversaries or special achievements.

• KITE You are restless, yet hopeful of a new direction or inspiration to show you the way. Remain open-minded and do not rule anything out. Your desire for novelty and worthwhile challenges will attract new experiences, so be brave and see which way the wind blows. You might be pleasantly surprised by the results.

• HORSESHOE A lucky horseshoe is protective and positive under any circumstances, and is especially so if you are planning a trip of any kind.

• QUESTION MARK Obviously, this means that you have an important question to ask, or that you will soon be questioning some part of your life. Nearby symbols should offer guidance, or reveal how long you must wait for an answer. If there are none, cultivate patience and remain open-minded.

• EXCLAMATION MARK This may indicate a surprise, or act as a warning against hasty actions or impulsive decisions. Either way, relax and maintain your routines. This is no time for risk-taking, remain cautious and all will be well.

• MERMAID The playful, childlike qualities of your personality come to the fore now as creativity and humor bubble up, heralding an inventive or artistic phase. Alternatively, a trip to the sea may be signified, but only if you see travel or nautical symbols lying beside the mermaid.

• UNICORN *Take your wishes, hopes and dreams seriously when this magical creature visits your cup. If you are prone to limiting yourself, your imagination, or your ideas it is time to write a wish list, study visualization techniques, and think big.*

• DRAGON *Something may not be what it seems in your life, as the dragon is master of illusion, trickery and showmanship. Beware 'get–rich–quick' schemes, flashy strangers and seductive acquaintances when this creature appears. You can enjoy the show, but do not get taken in.*

This may also be significant if the inquirer was born in the Chinese year of the dragon.

• FAIRIES *Fairies bring possibilities and opportunities, sometimes in disguise, and often out of the blue. Such possibilities are often small, subtle or even unlikely – much like fairy gifts in the old stories. But success and happiness often hide in such opportunities, so do not ignore them. Fairies are notoriously capricious, and a chance missed or rejected now could be cause for regret later on, when you will realize your mistake.*

• ANGEL *An angel is always a powerful symbol of protection from harm, and frequently heralds good news, especially if you have been waiting to hear from someone or are anxious to know how they are. An angel reduces or negates difficult or unpleasant symbols in your cup. Even if something negative occurs, you will not suffer as a result.*

• BALLOON *Fun and parties are the meaning of this symbol, but be careful not to waste all of your energy in socializing. You may be unable to settle down if this symbol appears close to the handle. An* initial *nearby suggests that someone in your life is afraid of commitment to a job or relationship. Otherwise, simply anticipate a forthcoming busy social phase and enjoy yourself.*

 ◆ **DICE** *A sure sign that fate is poised to take a hand, dice are strictly neutral symbols of change. Nearby signs should reveal to you what kind of changes, but sometimes you will find it difficult to identify them. Allow destiny to prevail and go with the flow. Matters will turn out well.*

◆ **MONEY SIGNS** *Money symbols mean lump sums of money usually, rather than a salary increase. They represent lottery wins, inheritances, cash payments or insurance money. Generally, there should be enough to have some fun with, as well as undertaking sensible plans and investment schemes.*

 ◆ **FIREWORKS** *Creative energy can be channelled into any area of your life, you do not have to be artistic to create a lively environment or start your own business. Fireworks encourage you to make a start, however small. Help and encouragement will follow.*

◆ **MUSICAL INSTRUMENTS** *In general, all musical instruments suggest a love of music, and usually some talent. They can sometimes symbolize a musical career or a musician in your life, especially when linked to an initial or human face. In this case, music is very important, so look carefully to see precisely why.*

◆ **HAT** *A hat means success, generally, but usually signifies that you will be 'wearing a different hat' as the saying goes. This might mean a new job, getting married or simply developing new skills or a new hobby. The* only exception to this interpretation is when a hat is accompanied by an initial or is actually on a head. Then it signifies a visitor or guest who could make quite an impact on you. This may indicate a new romance, job or friendship. But do not go overboard until you identify other relevant symbols nearby.

◆ SHOES *You are on the right path, but need some help, praise or encouragement to keep going.* Just be careful who you ask, gossip or negative influences can accompany this sign. Knowing you are heading in the right direction is sometimes all the help you need for now, so just keep going.

◆ WREATH *A wreath is a symbol of loss, but do not interpret a death – this is irresponsible, and besides, you are more than likely to* be mistaken. Loss of money, prestige or a relationship are more typical manifestations of this symbol.

◆ BOX *Look closely – is it a box, or is it just a square or rectangular shape? If it is a box, you are about to* receive a gift, within the time zone specified by its position. This is always a welcome present.

◆ FAN *Once upon a time everyone carried a fan, making this a common symbol in Victorian and Edwardian* readings, but nowadays they are more unusual. A fan describes someone who enjoys flirtation, and has a light–hearted attitude.

◆ TRIDENT *A symbol of the sea, the trident was the mythical weapon of the ancient Greek god of the oceans, Poseidon –* known to the Romans as Neptune. This powerful symbol used to mean that someone close to you was joining the Navy – and clearly in certain cases it still does. But its significance is much broader, and it should be interpreted as the mysterious pull of the ocean beckoning you to the seashore. Perhaps you will make a meaningful voyage by sea or spend some time beside it. A simple walk by the sea could clear your head or bring inspiration. Why not take a trip? Whatever happens will be memorable, fulfilling and possibly even fateful.

• ACORN The old adage 'big oak trees from little acorns grow', should give you an idea of the positive vitality that is symbolized by this emblem. Traditionally, the acorn means good health and prosperity, but it also denotes longstanding circumstances which will continue to bring happiness and contentment into your life. This is a fortunate symbol to find – even if circumstances are bleak now, they will soon improve with enduring results.

• SKULL You might be alarmed to find this rather stark image in your cup, but there is no need. A skull simply symbolizes

brainpower, intellectual effort, and a period of intensive mental work or study.

• BONES The bones of a story, creature or human being are its support structure. Bones mean inner support, strength and the essence of your character. Your strength may well be challenged or tested, but it will prove to be more than equal to anything you can encounter now, To discover the nature of this test look alongside the bones for clues. A heart, for example, would mean that a relationship is entering a difficult phase. A bird might suggest some important news that requires an immediate, practical response. Be confident of your strength and stand firm.

• FEATHER A feather is a complex symbol to interpret, so assess the surrounding images carefully before you decide what it means. Truth and justice are currently important in your life, but unstable circumstances may be working against you and it could be some time before you can achieve more balance. This may apply to your love life, job, friendships or financial circumstances. At the time of the reading things are in a state of flux like a feather floating on the breeze, so proceed slowly and do not make rash decisions.

◆ HOURGLASS *(Egg timer)* Time is running out, and you must act swiftly or lose out on something you desire. Living in the past or putting things on hold will have negative results now. Specific situations will be revealed by nearby results. Seize the moment or you may regret it.

◆ SWORD *A sword suggests conflicts, quarrels and disputes, often due to different ideas or principles between you or your inquirer and another. Physical conflicts are never symbolized by swords, these* battles are always conducted on the neutral plane. Each adversary firmly believes he or she is right. You may need an impartial point of view from a third party when this argumentative symbol appears.

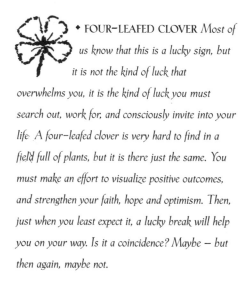

◆ FOUR-LEAFED CLOVER *Most of us know that this is a lucky sign, but it is not the kind of luck that* overwhelms you, it is the kind of luck you must search out, work for, and consciously invite into your life. A four-leafed clover is very hard to find in a field full of plants, but it is there just the same. You must make an effort to visualize positive outcomes, and strengthen your faith, hope and optimism. Then, just when you least expect it, a lucky break will help you on your way. Is it a coincidence? Maybe – but then again, maybe not.

◆ FLAG *A flag demands attention, and acts as a warning sign, bringing your attention to something important in your life.*

Whatever it is will be revealed by nearby pictures, and usually involves a question of principles. Perhaps you are about to get involved with a scheme, project or relationship that has hidden dangers, pitfalls or drawbacks. A cautious, pragmatic approach, plus some hard-headed thinking is required now. Do not worry about missing out; as the old Scottish saying goes, 'What's for you won't go past you.'

♦ PEN *Written communication is about to be meaningful or very important in your life. This symbol often appears in the readings of writers, authors and others who deal with words on a daily basis as part of their profession. An* initial *nearby, for example, would suggest that you are about to meet someone like this. Or, perhaps you have creative writing skills yourself? A pen linked to any warning symbol means that you will receive a letter or e-mail which upsets you. A pen linked to something positive means that some very good news is heading your way.*

♦ THRONE *Power and authority are entering your life in some form. Usually, a throne means promotion, success or the fulfilment of an ambition you have pursued for a long time. Sometimes it means that you will be meeting someone influential, such as the head of a large company, a celebrity, or someone with important connections. Surrounding symbols and the overall atmosphere of the pictures you see, must be read alongside such a dramatic image.*

♦ PARACHUTE *You are poised to jump into the unknown, and it may feel like a huge risk or a foolish gamble. But a parachute shows that you are, in fact, doing the right thing at the right time. Circumstances and helpful people will ensure you make a safe landing, even though you may be feeling a little out of control or nervous. There is really nothing to fear. If you feel anxious, remember the spiritual maxim, 'leap and the net will appear' – and make that jump.*

◆ PIPE *A pipe denotes deep contemplation, and through its traditional role in many tribal cultures it symbolizes peace and resolution in any situation where there have been arguments or differences of opinion. That famous fictional detective, Sherlock Holmes, used to smoke his pipe whenever he was mulling over some complex web of tantalizing clues. Native Americans would smoke a peace pipe in a ritual designed to mark the end of a conflict. You may need some quiet moments to yourself, but you will be able to resolve a troublesome dilemma in the time zone indicated by its place in the cup.*

◆ SCALES *Scales mean balance, justice and equality. If something in your life is imbalanced, the scales show that you are aware of this and are about to take action to remedy the situation. Perhaps you are spending too much time at work, and not enough time with friends or loved ones? Perhaps you could be developing your skills and creative gifts? Perhaps you are involved with a lawsuit, and hoping for justice? Whatever the circumstances, the scales suggest that a fair and balanced outcome will eventually satisfy you.*

When accompanied by an initial *or a* face, *scales can represent someone born under the sign of* Libra.

Astrological Symbols

Animals, creatures and figures can refer to signs of the zodiac or Chinese horoscope signs, but generally this is only true when you are already familiar with such things or are studying them seriously. If this is the case refer to the following list of Western and Eastern symbols. You can use them for inspiration or enlightenment if you feel this is the right thing to do. However, do not 'mix and match' the interpretations given earlier with the astrological symbols unless you are experienced. Even then you will achieve better results if you clearly separate the traditional meanings given earlier in the book from the astrological ones which follow. Novice readers should only use these interpretations if the sign appears beside a symbol which describes a person, such as an initial, face or body shape.

Western astrology allocates one symbolic creature, figure or object to each sign of the zodiac, for example, the ram symbolizes the sign of Aries. Some of the symbols or glyphs associated with the signs of the zodiac, which are also featured on the *Cup of Destiny* saucer, are complex and unlikely to be formed by tea leaves or coffee grounds. Others are simple shapes that could well appear, such as the arrow of Sagittarius.

Your intuition should help you to decide whether those wavy lines describe the sea or indicate the sign Aquarius. Is that a pillar or the symbol for Gemini? Reading a cup is always an intuitive, right–brain process, so do not become anxious about what is 'right'. The less attached you are to such concepts the better. Relax; allow your imagination to lead you and your intuition will do the rest.

SIGNS OF THE ZODIAC

ARIES

21 March – 20 April

Key words: Vital, impulsive, leader

Element: Fire

Symbolized by the ram, Aries is the first sign of the zodiac, and is believed to be the sign of a soul on its first journey through the twelve signs of the year. Aries people possess childlike qualities, such as naive enthusiasm and impulsive reactions. They are quick to fall in and out of love with people, careers or locations. But honesty and lack of guile makes it easy to forgive them, while their energy and positivity means that they are often successful.

Speed and clarity are very important to Arians, but few can match their ability to forge ahead. Their impatience can be a problem. Overall Aries people are exciting and stimulating friends and unforgettable romantic partners.

TAURUS

21 April – 21 May

Key words: Practical, sensual, stubborn

Element: Earth

Taurus, symbolized by a bull, is the sign of the builder. They rarely enjoy change and prefer lasting relationships, both personally and professionally. A powerful attachment to the material world means that they enjoy sensual pleasures such as good food, fine wines and perfumes. Creating a comfortable home is of paramount importance, and earning sufficient money to indulge themselves is perhaps even more vital to their happiness and well-being. But practicality masks a deeply romantic nature, and the true Taurean makes a passionate, if unimaginative, lover, and a warm, affectionate long-term partner. They can be very appealing to other less stable personalities.

GEMINI

22 May – 21 June

Key words: Communicative, restless, witty

Element: Air

Ⅱ *Symbolized by twins, the first air sign of the zodiac js the sign of paradox, contrast and quick-witted responses to the world about them. Within every Gemini you will find at least two distinct personalities, sometimes more. The talkative, amusing and charming social face of a Gemini is only one facet of a complex and sometimes moody personality. Geminis need more mental stimulation and variety than any other sign in the zodiac. When bored, they become restless and unreliable, or need periods of time alone. They are flirtatious and seductive in love, but again, easily bored or distracted. Geminis make excellent friends and fine company, however.*

CANCER

22 June – 22 July

Key words: Maternal, soft-hearted, protective

Element: Water

The Cancerian personality is accurately symbolized by the crab, *for they are frequently tough outside and soft and vulnerable within. Protective of those they love, they are equally self-protective and this trait applies to both love and their professional interests. Cancerians find it hard to let anything or anyone go, and consequently make great collectors of both friends and beautiful objects. This is the most maternal, nurturing sign, but such warm and tender emotions are not bestowed on everyone. It can take a long time to win the love and loyalty of somone born under this sign.*

LEO

23 July – 23 August

Key words: Sunny, dramatic, exuberant

Element: Fire

♌ Symbolized by a lion, the second fire sign of the zodiac is renowned for its vitality and sense of drama, as well as its obstinate determination to make an impact on those around it. Often ambitious, a Leo must have some creative outlet, somewhere to shine, or they become morose and frustrated. A sense of fun and playful characteristics similarly need expression, or all that warmth and energy dissolves.

Romantic and flirtatious, Leos love to love and are usually loyal to friends and partners. From time to time they hear the call of the wild and must roam the jungle. A happy Leo rarely disappears for long, however. Leos make firm friends and generous lovers, but once betrayed they can be as cold and dangerous as any Scorpio.

VIRGO

24 August – 23 September

Key words: Organized, meticulous, critical

Element: Earth

♍ Virgo is symbolized by a maiden carrying a sheaf of corn. There is something refined about a typical Virgo, even in their boisterous or extrovert moments. This is traditionally the sign of service to others, and Virgoans are often found working in health care or one of the other caring professions. They are witty and discerning with a finely tuned critical eye and excellent taste. While sometimes critical of others, they are also self-critical perfectionists who can worry needlessly about the smallest detail. In love they are often equally demanding, and may have difficulty in intimate relationships as others rarely live up to their high standards. They are loyal, however, and often very kind and thoughtful.

LIBRA

24 September – 23 October

Key words: Charming, manipulative, artistic

Element: Air

Symbolized by a pair of scales, *it is the only sign to be represented by an object. Librans value balance very highly. This is the sign of relationships, but all Libran relationships must contain a strong mental rapport or they will founder and fail. Librans are charming flirts, because they enjoy the mental exercise. They are suspicious of grand passions since these are imbalanced and out of control. Companionship is more important for them, both in love and at work. Librans rarely work well alone, and many hate to live alone too. They are artistic, extravagant, and have a natural sense of justice and harmony.*

SCORPIO

24 October – 22 November

Key words: Intense, secretive, curious

Element: Water

Symbolized by a scorpion, and inextricably linked with the deepest questions of human existence, Scorpio is said to be the most mysterious and intense sign. Their affinity with mystery, and their desire to solve puzzles, leads many to become gifted researchers, detectives, or psychotherapists, exploring the labyrinths of the unconscious mind. They have great reserves of strength and can be ruthless, relentless and dedicated. In love they are equally focussed, preferring passion to casual friendship and deep conversation to lightweight banter. A need for secrecy and control means that they rarely – if ever –reveal all their thoughts and feelings. They are extremely loyal once won, but it takes a long time and many tests before they will accept you.

SAGITTARIUS

23 November – 21 December

Key words: Humorous, philosophical, adventurous

Element: Fire

Symbolized by a centaur or archer, free-spirited Sagittarians are blessed with amazing optimism and faith in the future. Their positive outlook attracts good fortune, and numerous friends but they can become depressed if things prove too challenging. Extroverted and good-humored, they are fond of socializing, sport and travel. Many have a close relationship with animals, working with them or keeping them as pets. Human relationships need more work, however, as their need for freedom can conflict with their need for love and companionship. Many settle down quite late in life, others flit from one relationship to another, and never confront their fear of commitment. They make inspirational friends, as well as marvellous party guests.

CAPRICORN

22 December – 20 January

Key words: Patient, ambitious, well-organized

Element: Earth

Capricorn is symbolized by a goat with a fish tail. Practical and pragmatic, Capricorns tend to prefer an orderly existence and a well-organized routine. They do, however, possess a hidden side which they keep under wraps until they trust you. They are as sensuous as any Taurean, and can be extravagant and pleasure-loving. Typically, Capricorns are careful with their resources – this includes cash, companions, skills and any area of life where they have invested time or energy. But they have a weakness for luxury, good-quality items and well-made clothing. They are, like their opposite sign Cancer, slow to trust but loyal and steadfast once they have allowed you into their secret hearts.

AQUARIUS

21 January – 19 February

Key words: Humanitarian, analytical,

inventive

Element: Air

Aquarius is symbolized by a figure pouring water from a vase, showing the sign's need to contain emotion and benefit all – signified by the action of watering the earth. Humanitarian impulses and a desire to inform, uplift or reform some aspect of life typify this sign.

They are ambitious, but their aims and objectives may be unconventional or eccentric. Like Librans and Geminis they prize mental rapport above other qualities in friendship or love, although their need for stability and security is greater than their fellow air signs. Within any close friendship or love relationship they need freedom and a certain amount of space for their own thoughts. They make stimulating friends and relatively undemanding long-term partners.

PISCES

20 February – 20 March

Key words: Imaginative, sensitive, private

Element: Water

Symbolized by two fish swimming in opposite directions, Pisces is said to contain a little of each of the preceeding signs, plus a generous helping of intuition and visionary flair. Pisceans can be ultra-sensitive, but shy away from circumstances or people that threaten their inner world. They are private rather than secretive, and combine vulnerability with strong survival instincts. Many Pisceans become successful, but none can take the glare of the spotlight for long periods. Like fish, they need to hide away from time to time to restore their sense of well-being. Highly romantic, Pisceans learn to mask their feelings early in life. They can be unfaithful and unreliable, but this springs from a need to protect themselves, rather than any desire to hurt another person.

CHINESE ASTROLOGY

If Chinese astrology is meaningful for you you might like to use it to identify an individual in the cup. A quick guide to each animal in the twelve-year cycle follows.

RAT

Key words: Intelligent, active, charming

Element: Water

 Individuals born in the year of the Rat need security. They are passionate, faithful and loyal, but can be critical and when others disappoint them in love or business.

OX

Key words: Quiet, steady, gentle

Element: Earth

 Individuals born in the year of the Ox tend to be as determined as any bull, and indeed have much in common with the Western *zodiac sign, Taurus. Ox people need friends and partners, whose vitality is rewarded with tolerance and great loyalty.*

TIGER

Key words: Positive, enthusiastic, determined

Element: Wood

 Vibrant optimists, Tiger people relish excitement and thrive on adventure and challenge. They can be fickle in love, needing romance and independence more than stability. While generous, Tigers can also be obstinate.

RABBIT

Key words: Intelligent, imaginative, sensitive

Element: Wood

 Every Rabbit needs a safe haven of tranquil harmony; these individuals focus on creating tender relationships and elegant

surroundings. *They are sometime shy, leading to misunderstandings with others, but are caring and thoughtful nonetheless.*

DRAGON

Key words: Charismatic, lively, self-confident

Element: Earth

 Dragons embrace life with whole-hearted enthusiasm, bravery and amazing energy. They are volatile and attractive, but can be ruthless and impatient with weaker individuals. They enjoy intense experiences.

SNAKE

Key words: Decisive, active, courageous

Element: Fire

 Snakes have an inbuilt desire for free-dom, while expecting others to remain loyal. Their charm can be irresistible, but they can take a long time to trust friends or lovers.

HORSE

Key words: Independent, confident, cheerful

Element: Fire

 Outgoing, outspoken and hungry for intellectual inspiration, Horses are impulsive creatures. Excited by new discoveries, they find it hard to keep a secret. They are playful, quick-tempered, and make exciting partners in love, business or friendship.

RAM

Key words: Emotional, considerate, creative

Element: Earth

 Dreamy, imaginative free spirits, those born in the year of the Ram dislike restrictive circumstances or relationships. They also have the nature of a wanderer, and are happy to set off around the world to meet people. But their sensitivity means that an understanding partner is essential to their well-being.

MONKEY

Key words: Versatile, intelligent, good-humored

Element: Metal

Adaptable Monkeys appear to be light-hearted and flirtatious, but have tender hearts and sympathetic natures. As playful as their symbolic animal, they are also shrewd and cunning. Never underestimate them.

ROOSTER

Key words: Logical, straightforward, charming

Element: Metal

Self-confident Roosters appear lively and extremely independent, and enjoy a varied and social romantic life. Yet beneath this veneer, Roosters can be compassionate, creative and persevering. They may be exhibitionists, but there is also a wise, brave side when needed.

DOG *Key words:* Dedicated, honest, courageous

Element: Earth

Dogs have a great talent for friendships and enduring associations but need plenty of reassurance before they trust others. Once won over, they are fiercely protective towards those they love. Their search for truth can make them over-critical, but they are rarely misled by appearances or the superficial.

PIG

Key words: Affectionate, hard-working, reflective

Element: Water

Their childlike qualities can land Pigs in sticky situations as they tend to act first and think later. They look for the best in people. Their sense of fun wins admirers, and they are affectionate partners.

PART THREE

SAMPLE READINGS

The four sample readings on the following pages have been included to demonstrate how a real-life session unfolds, and how certain important themes seem to appear in various guises. Gathering these picture-symbols together and creating a story reveals individual concerns and coming events. By looking at the cup as a whole, as well as identifying individual signs, you will be able to make a satisfying reading for yourself or for your friends.

Sample Reading: Katie

This is a reading for Katie, a successful single woman in her early thirties. Katie is basically satisfied and happy with her life, but has been feeling restless and unsettled for no obvious reason. She is ready for a change of some kind, and wants to see what the future might bring.

When the coffee is poured there are lots of bubbles on the surface of the liquid signifying that Katie is about to receive some extra money. This turns to be correct – she is expecting a tax refund any day.

Once she has spun and drained her cup some liquid still remains, suggesting a little sadness in her life, despite her outer confidence and positive outlook. But, it seems, future events will soon banish her feelings of unhappiness; *there are some intriguing symbols close to the rim and the immediate future looks lively.*

The first symbol, closest to the rim of the cup, is a mountain, beside a hat and a wavy line.

A visitor is denoted by the hat, while the wavy line means that Katie has an emotional reaction and link to this person. The mountain, while demonstrating Katie's determination and ambitious qualities, are most likely to be describing an actual location. Katie is puzzled at first, but then she remembers that her ex-boyfriend is travelling in Switzerland. Their relationship, although friendly, still remains 'unfinished business', and they had parted some six months ago because neither felt ready for a more serious commitment. So what might his visit bring?

A little further down the cup we see a large question mark *next to an arch. There are also* two circles *nearby, and a large number of* random dots. There will be an opportunity to travel, signified by

the arch, plus a gift and the possibility of some extra cash – already hinted at by the bubbles on the surface when the cup was full.

It seems as if Katie's boyfriend has had a change of heart, but it is too soon to predict a revival of their romance. The question mark means that Katie must ask herself if this is what she wants or whether she must decide to move on and leave the past behind. With travel so strongly emphasized in this cup, a trip could be the catalyst she needs – with or without her man. Generally, this looks like a positive turning point, and she will not have to wait too long either.

QUESTION MARK

TWO CIRCLES

ARCH

WAVY LINE

HAT

MOUNTAIN

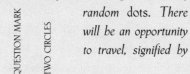

Sample Reading: Ellen

Ellen has a birthday coming up, and is feeling lonely. She specifically wants to ask about her love life, which is non-existent. She focuses on this question while drinking her tea, and asks for some guidance and news about her chances as she spins the cup. This is what the symbols reveal:

A heart *appears right on the rim of the cup, close to the handle. This confirms Ellen's focus on her question, and reassures her too. The heart signifies that love is not far away, since she is open and ready to receive it.*

Other symbols lie scattered around the base and on the bottom of the cup. Ellen will have to be patient for little while longer – perhaps a month or two. But a perfect circle *promises luck and perhaps a gift. And this is just beginning. Right at the bottom of the cup is a* horse, *describing Ellen's inner strength and patience –*

qualities she will need in the coming weeks. It may also signify a Sagittarian *person coming into her life – and as she asked about a partner, this could be that person's birth sign. Curiously enough, there is also an* arrow *in Ellen's reading, which affirms this possibility.*

An ivy leaf nearby encourages Ellen to ask for support from friends. Someone she knows could help in her romantic quest. Close by we find a spiral, *signifying Ellen's creative energy and potent intuitive gifts. If she stops trying so hard, and uses her abilities to guide her she will soon know whether she is on the right path.*

In the very bottom of the cup is a parasol *and the* number two. *Ellen is protected and can now move towards a more loving and romantic phase with complete confidence. The number confirms the message of the cup's pattern; there is a little way to go before she achieves her heart's desire, probably about two months.*

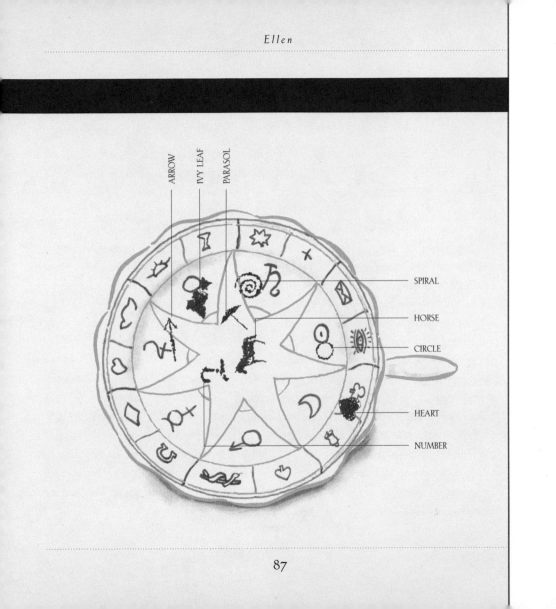

ARROW

IVY LEAF

PARASOL

SPIRAL

HORSE

CIRCLE

HEART

NUMBER

Sample reading: Daniel

Daniel is at a crossroads in his life, and is wondering whether to relocate, make significant career changes, pursue a new relationship, or simply wait and see.

His cup is unusually full of symbols, indicating an important phase in his life. But Daniel's calm demeanor hides an anxious spirit, signified by a lizard close to the handle and a face. He is thinking too much, and worrying unnecessarily. A rectangle confirms the challenges he is facing, but a flower by the rim shows that he is well-appreciated in his personal and professional life. Daniel must make an effort to relax, or he will find it difficult to make beneficial changes, since tension tends to cut us off from our intuition and inner guidance.

Further warning signs are the X-shaped cross and exclamation mark, side by side. Daniel cannot continue on his present path, in his current state of anxiety. His stress levels are blocking creative solutions to his dilemmas, as well as posing a health risk.

Fortunately, there are some exciting and uplifting symbols for him to focus on. A bow means some kind of gift or celebration, while a key reveals that Daniel's life may take a turn for the better in the weeks to come. Close to the key we find an airplane, some straight lines and a question mark. A long trip looks likely, and the lines indicate that it will be a satisfying and successful one. Relocation may not be likely in the near future, but an exploratory trip could answer Daniel's questions, or even inspire other options.

The triangle sits alone, promising luck, and an unexpected boost of some kind. A crown clearly shows that Daniel's professional reputation is growing, and heralds some positive recognition or public success.

And what about his love life? With several symbols suggesting admiration, or gifts (flower, bow, crown), Daniel should be feeling popular and appreciated. Fire promises passion, but there are no clues about its source, such as an initial or heart symbol. It is possible that he has yet to meet the person who is the cause of this emotion, or that his feelings will intensify within his present relationship. However, the triangle and the exclamation mark both suggest he would be wise to expect the unexpected in all departments. Once he learns how to relax and be flexible he can open the door to some magical experiences, and enjoy the challenges life is about to throw at him.

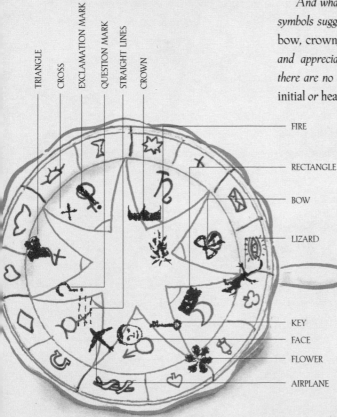

TRIANGLE

CROSS

EXCLAMATION MARK

QUESTION MARK

STRAIGHT LINES

CROWN

FIRE

RECTANGLE

BOW

LIZARD

KEY

FACE

FLOWER

AIRPLANE

Sample Reading Four: Susy

Susy is curious about her immediate future, and is particularly interested in her job prospects. She is also going through an awkward patch in her relationship, which is the cause of some tension.

Three interlinked circles *appear close to the rim, suggesting general good fortune and perhaps a gift. There is a tiny* mermaid *beside the largest of the three circles, a symbol of joy and a reminder of the sea – an important point, as we shall see.*

An unbroken line of pictures appears, all the way down to the bottom of the cup, signifying an unfolding chain of events and possibly a journey. It is interesting to see a trident *at the very bottom, another symbol linked with the sea – connecting beautifully with the mermaid at the top. The seaside is about to figure in Susy's life, although the presence of an* exclamation mark *at the bottom of the cup denotes a surprise. Since she is not planning to visit the coast, this makes sense.*

Her career concerns will be answered in a week to ten days' time; towards the bottom of the cup we see a flying bird, *signifying good news, and an* arch *– denoting an opportunity – beside a tall* building. *The building means success through hard work, and shows that Susy has already laid firm foundations for a fulfilling future.*

And what about her love life? The bubbles, *symbolize fun, frivolity and parties. A* triangle *in the bottom of the cup promises good luck too; she won't be bored but will she find personal happiness? A* heart *is found at the bottom, plus the* initials D and M. *Her boyfriend's name is Michael, but the D is a mystery initial. With all the socializing indicated by her cup, she may meet someone else. A* cross *nearby signifies problems and delays; she may be entering a turbulent phase but the cup's general air of good fortune shows she can handle it with aplomb. By remembering the mermaid's joyful, feminine qualities she can enjoy an intriguing couple of weeks and soon expand her horizons.*

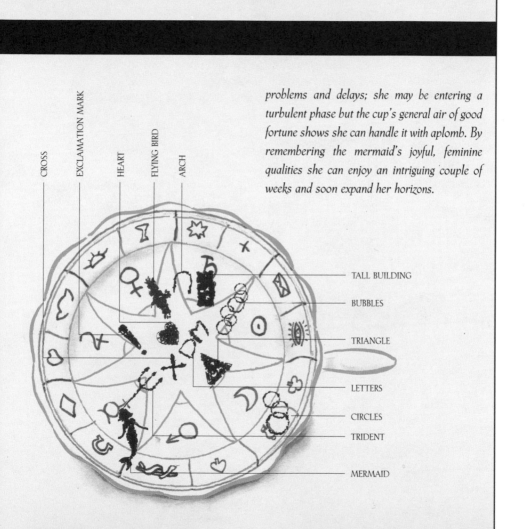

CROSS

EXCLAMATION MARK

HEART

FLYING BIRD

ARCH

TALL BUILDING

BUBBLES

TRIANGLE

LETTERS

CIRCLES

TRIDENT

MERMAID

Index

Acknowledgements

Author's acknowledgements

I would like to thank the team at Eddison Sadd Editions for making this long-cherished project possible; especially Ian Jackson, Nick Eddison, Liz Wheeler, Nicky Hodgson and Pritty Ramjee. And to those who offered me support, fun and chocolate during the creative process, my heartfelt thanks.

EDDISON • SADD EDITIONS

Eddison Sadd Editions acknowledge with grateful thanks Aynsley China Limited, Stoke-on-Trent, England for their kind permission to reproduce their stunning original 'Nelros Cup of Fortune' design.

COMMISSIONING EDITOR	*Liz Wheeler*
EDITOR	*Nicola Hodgson*
INDEXER	*Dorothy Frame*
PROOFREADER	*Mary Lambert*
ART DIRECTOR	*Elaine Partington*
SENIOR ART EDITOR	*Pritty Ramjee*
PRODUCTION	*Charles James, Karyn Claridge*